CROSSING PATHS
Reading Hands for Love and Work

by
VERNON MAHABAL

Hand Illustrations by
TIM LUKOWIAK

Edited by
ND KOSTER

MANDALA
PUBLISHING

SAN RAFAEL, CA

©2004 MANDALA PUBLISHING
TEXT ©2004 VERNON MAHABAL
ALL RIGHTS RESERVED
DESIGNED BY INSIGHT DESIGN
PRINTED IN CHINA THROUGH PALACE PRESS INTERNATIONAL

10 9 8 7 6 5 4 3 2 1

LIBRARY OF CONGRESS CATALOGING-IN-PUBLICATION DATA IS AVAILABLE.

ISBN 1-932771-17-4

CONTENTS

5   PREFACE

7   INTRODUCTION

8   THE DIFFERENCE BETWEEN THE TWO HANDS

9   HOW TO USE THIS BOOK

10   MAP OF THE HAND

11   TRAIT GUIDE

13   *Love*

57   WORK

96   A NOTE FROM THE AUTHOR

Crossing Paths is a guide for pinpointing the talents, abilities and potential of those whom you have, or may be considering having, some form of relationship with. It gives you the ability to identify people's essential qualities and characteristics, which in turn allows you to better understand and work with your family, friends, lovers, co-workers and business associates.

Within the context of a complete palmistry consultation, numerous features and elements are taken into consideration simultaneously and analyzed in relation to each other. The interpretations contained within this book focus on specific features in isolation. Nevertheless, their meanings stand firm and are not diminished by supplementary or contrasting influences.

While it generally takes months or even years to ascertain a person's nature, this book will assist you in immediately assessing your relationships without having to endure the lengthy study typically associated with such disciplines. You now have a tool to identify an individual's underlying traits and motivations, which gives you a tremendous advantage in gauging how to best interact and enjoy the relationship. Similarly, if someone informs you that they carry a particular personality trait, or possess a specific attribute, you now have an accurate and even entertaining system to verify it with certainty. Most importantly, this book is designed to be fun and easy to use!

INTRODUCTION

Palmistry is an ancient science and an unsurpassed tool for character and emotional analysis. The palmer surface of the human hand, by its very nature, contains vast amounts of detailed personal information. Everyone has the ability to tap its potential for insight, reflection and greater mutual understanding. Responsible and serious practitioners have published numerous palmistry books over the past century. However, the great majority of these texts are not well suited for today's readers. Unlike its predecessors, *Crossing Paths* brings this complex, Old World method into the hands of modern, everyday inquirers.

Crossing Paths is a powerful reference and resource guide for those who want a quick, accurate way to assess their partner's talents, abilities, psychology and emotional personality. You need not have an interest in palmistry in order to use this book; the underlying concepts, methodology and philosophy of hand analysis have been purposely left out. The diagrams and accompanying text are deliberately simple and straightforward, providing quick access to vital answers and potential solutions to pressing questions. The information found here is based upon extensive background research and years of practice working with thousands of people. Although it has not been written with the intention of producing a professional palmist, an experienced palmist will nonetheless find, within these pages, much advanced and interesting material to add to their study.

The left, or "objective," brain transmits its portfolio and recorded information to the right hand. The right, or "subjective," brain transmits its dossier to the left hand. Therefore, the general rule is that the right hand symbolizes the outer (or applied) self, and the left hand symbolizes the inner (or emotional) self. This holds true for left-handers also.

When you examine a pair of hands, concentrate primarily on the right hand, as this will chronicle the actual reality and present state of affairs in a person's life. The left hand, correspondingly, will show potential and what is internally wished for and desired. Comparing both hands together will give you the most comprehensive indicator of how a person will act and interact within relationships.

Let's say you want to know if your partner is a good listener. Look up the words in the Trait Guide, turn to the corresponding page and view the diagram. The diagram will reveal the strongest sign of listening skills found in the hand.

Now observe both of your partner's hands in order to see if either hand contains the configuration. A match-up will indicate that mediation, for instance, is a strong talent and that it can be used powerfully and effectively. Always keep in mind that whenever a match-up occurs, the quality indicated by that specific configuration will play an evident role in that person's life.

You will also find the names of well-known characters or public figures included with each entry. These are representative only. The author has included them for your inspiration and to assist in identifying the traits in question. Each individual has been carefully selected because their public identity has become synonymous with certain personality traits, and indeed, one would expect to find the corresponding configurations on their hands. No such claim, however, is made here that any specific corresponding configurations can or will be found.

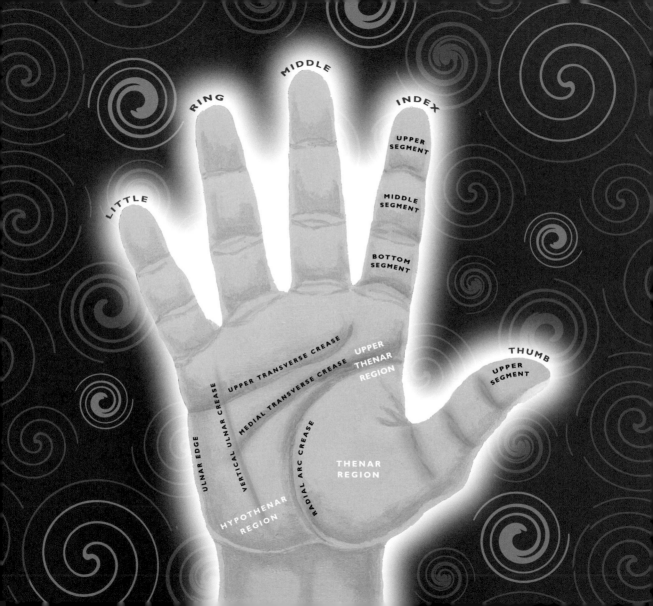

Love

WORK

Good Listener	14
Family-Oriented	16
Money-Making Ability	18
Faith in a Higher Power	20
Loyal	22
Good Friend	24
Aggressive	26
Open-Minded	28
Humorous	30
Warm-Hearted	32
Emotionally Reserved	34
Sex Drive	36
Fun-Loving	38
Selfish	40
Demonstrative	42
Manipulative	44
Superficial	46
Pessimistic	48
Philosophical	50
Passionate	52
Refined	54

Cooking Ability	58
Nature Lover	60
Adventurous	62
Opinionated	64
Honest	66
Dishonest	68
Ambitious	70
Independent	72
Decision-maker	74
Visionary	76
Strong-willed	78
Imaginative	80
Creative	82
Analytical	84
Intelligent	86
Money-making Ability	88
Communicative	90
Hard-working	92
Team Player	94

Good Listener

A person whose upper transverse crease is notable in length and straightness possesses excellent listening skills. Consequently, this line must forge a healthy incursion into the region beneath the index finger.

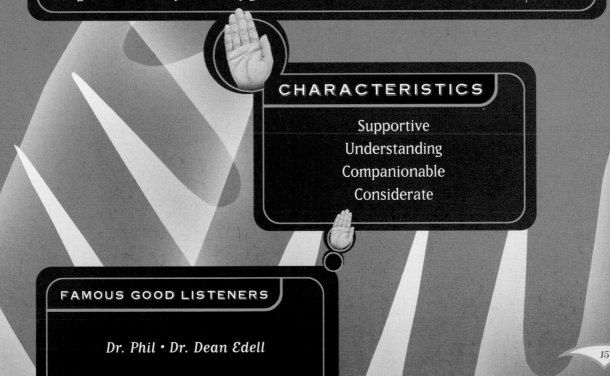

QUALITIES

This is the romantic idealist: a supportive person who can really listen when spoken to. Friends are always coming to them with their problems because they're assured of finding a sympathetic ear. If an argument erupts with this person, you can still expect them to consider your points with the temperament of a therapist. What's more, they're capable of making good, shared decisions. In general, they are very humanitarian and socially conscious. Sometimes they are taken advantage of, though, because they too freely give their time to others.

CHARACTERISTICS

Supportive
Understanding
Companionable
Considerate

FAMOUS GOOD LISTENERS

Dr. Phil • Dr. Dean Edell

15

Family-Oriented

A person who is family-oriented and who most likely embraces strong family connections will have a medial transverse crease that travels adjoined with the radial arc crease for a short distance at its commencement.

QUALITIES

This person understands the importance of family and appreciates traditional family values. They are not impulsive in domestic matters and will do everything within their power to keep their family together. They have an inherently strong family bond. For this reason, they respect and revere previous generations. On the downside, they may be so committed to this position that they remain in unsupportive marriages or relationships.

CHARACTERISTICS

Cautious
Strong Family Values
Conservative

FAMOUS FAMILY-ORIENTED PEOPLE

Bill Cosby • John Bradshaw

Money-Making Ability

*I*f the medial transverse crease draws up slightly toward the little finger as it ends its journey, it signifies a marked ability and desire to make a considerable amount of money. A spirit of competitiveness frequently accompanies this contour.

When it comes to money, this person just **gets** it. They have strong business acumen and they work hard to be successful. By nature they are pragmatic money-makers who enjoy playing the role of "provider." In general, they seize any opportunity that comes their way. This preoccupation, however, can prove quite consuming, and therefore these individuals may ignore other areas of their lives, such as health or spirituality.

CHARACTERISTICS

Good Provider
Strong Financial Management
Business Ability

FAMOUS MONEY-MAKERS

Suze Orman • Sam Walton

Faith in a Higher Power

When the upper segment of the index finger is visibly the longest of the three, you can expect to find a person with a strong belief and faith in the Divine. Further, an interest in actually taking up religious practices is strengthened if there are a few vertical lines etched into it, however faint.

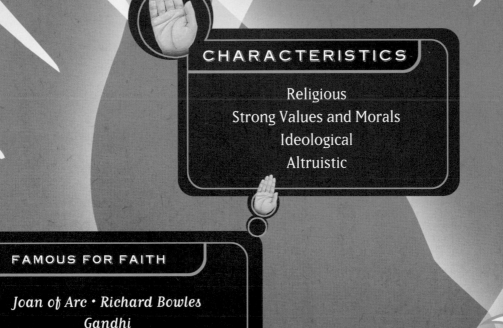

QUALITIES

People with this characteristic have an inborn, organic faith in God or the Goddess. They hold themselves to high standards. While harboring great expectations of others, they are not preachy. Yet, they are altruistic. In times of trouble, they remain surprisingly optimistic due to their conviction that a conscious, higher power with a meaningful plan is at work. Occasionally these individuals may become somewhat righteous or simply frustrated by the limitations they perceive others to be placing upon themselves.

CHARACTERISTICS

Religious
Strong Values and Morals
Ideological
Altruistic

FAMOUS FOR FAITH

Joan of Arc • Richard Bowles
Gandhi

Loyal

Although appearing somewhat short in length, this straight upper transverse crease ending underneath the region of the middle finger indicates a person who has an extremely loyal nature. This particular marking symbolizes the pinnacle of faithfulness.

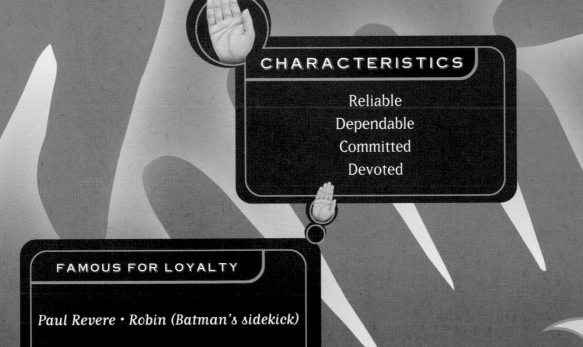

QUALITIES

Count on this person to be there for you—to exhibit unswerving devotion and dependability. Generally people with this crease don't fly head first into love, but instead pay close attention to their partner's actions and words and wait for them to prove themselves. Once they do, they're committed for the long term. They may have trouble expressing their feelings, however, and often need some time alone. Expect them to show their love through actions rather than words, as they have difficulty articulating what they feel. They are likely to give second chances, even after being betrayed.

CHARACTERISTICS

Reliable
Dependable
Committed
Devoted

FAMOUS FOR LOYALTY

Paul Revere · Robin (Batman's sidekick)

Good Friend

A person who values supportive friendships will have a rounded, upraised ball of the thumb, or thenar region. Moreover, a large and significantly elevated thenar pad indicates an abundance of charm and sincerity.

QUALITIES

This is the magnetic party guest—easy to meet and fun to be around. With a warm and personable disposition, this individual makes inviting and even entertaining company. On the downside, people with this feature tend to be impressionable and need to exercise some discrimination in order to avoid being manipulated.

CHARACTERISTICS

Friendly
Charming
Personable
Sincere

FAMOUS GOOD FRIENDS

Mister Rogers • Rachel Green

$\mathscr{E}$xamine the upper thenar region, the pad of flesh directly above the ball of the thumb. An inclination toward aggression is revealed by a slightly upraised and firm development of this region. Both the confirmation and the exacerbation of this quality are evidenced by a reddish hue and/or a few short and deeply engraved horizontal lines.

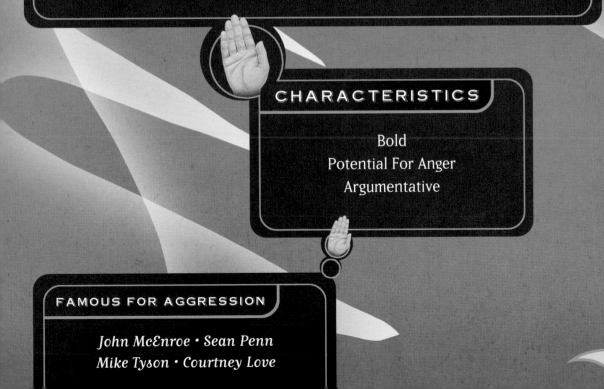

QUALITIES

This is the bold go-getter who takes the initiative to get things done. In a relationship, the person may have a tendency to be too forceful or obstinate. Therefore, they are more compatible with those of a similar nature who can reflect their aggressiveness back at them, helping them to recognize their misguided behavior and bring greater clarity to a given situation.

CHARACTERISTICS

Bold
Potential For Anger
Argumentative

FAMOUS FOR AGGRESSION

John McEnroe • Sean Penn
Mike Tyson • Courtney Love

Open~Minded

*L*ooking at the middle region of the palm, notice if there is a reasonably wide space between the upper and medial trans-verse creases. If so, it is a clear indicator of one who maintains an open mind on most topics.

LOVE

QUALITIES

These people are very accommodating in relationships. They are flexible, free spirits who approach life with a carefree and relaxed attitude. For them, the journey is more important than the destination. They are capable of seeing all sides of an argument, sometimes to a fault. This tendency leads them to be easily talked out of their own opinions, or fail to form their own opinions at all. They should be encouraged to take a stand in important matters, and to be less frivolous in general.

CHARACTERISTICS

Adaptable
Free-Spirited
Easy-Going

FAMOUS FOR OPEN-MINDEDNESS

Austin Powers • Dr. Wayne Dyer

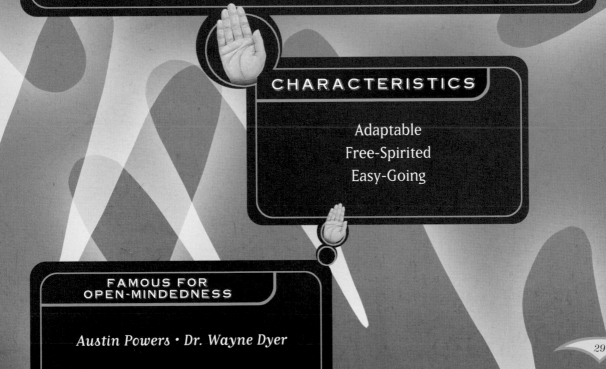

Humorous

People who are graced with a good sense of humor will bear a skin ridge pattern that occupies the ring and little finger interdigital space. This dermatoglyphic resembles a succession of arches within one another (1). An imprint that inclines toward the thumb at a 45° angle indicates a sense of humor that is sharply sarcastic and quick-witted (2).

1

2

QUALITIES

For these people, optimism springs from a quick wit. By seeing the inherent humor in life, they are able to rise above tough challenges and rebound from personal hardship. Men with this characteristic are always joking and laughing. Their partners may feel like everything is a joke, as though they're not being taken seriously enough. The negative aspect of this trait manifests when good humor turns bad—when harmless observations morph into scathing sarcasm or an unnecessarily cutting critique.

CHARACTERISTICS

Funny
Likes To Laugh
Witty

FAMOUS HUMORISTS

David Letterman • John Cleese
Lucille Ball

*A*n upper transverse crease that begins at the ulnar edge of the palm and ends in a gentle curve as it meets the base of the index finger reveals a warm-hearted nature.

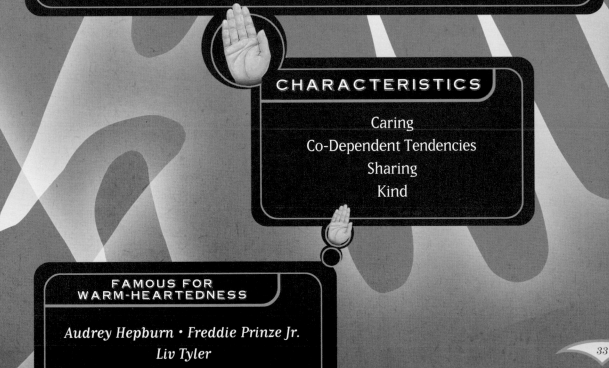

QUALITIES

This marking identifies the "nurturer" in relationships. These people are very giving, and will sacrifice their own needs to care for their partners. It is important to understand that they crave reciprocation too. They need to get back as much as they give, although they probably won't ask for it. Often they idealize their relationships while ignoring their practical experience. Therefore, they are prone to being taken advantage of and need to ask themselves if they are honestly getting what they need out of their relationships.

CHARACTERISTICS

Caring
Co-Dependent Tendencies
Sharing
Kind

FAMOUS FOR WARM-HEARTEDNESS

Audrey Hepburn • Freddie Prinze Jr.
Liv Tyler

One who displays an upper transverse crease that is predominantly linear in shape — regardless of its direction, depth or length — is reserved in the expression of their feelings and emotions.

QUALITIES

Think of these people as British, not Italian. It's not that they're unemotional, it's that they don't express their emotions in words. If an argument erupts, they may retreat into another room to cool off and think it through. They are patient people who keep the big picture in mind while weighing different sides of a discussion. They stay calm and deal with life in a mature way. To better understand their own feelings, however, they should make an effort to be more talkative, or at least to write down their thoughts.

CHARACTERISTICS

Shy
Passive
Even-Keeled
Patient

FAMOUS FOR EMOTIONAL RESTRAINT

Clint Eastwood • Diane Keaton

35

A deeply cut and possibly wide, dark looking radial arc crease is a sign of strong sexual drive. This crease is also likely to curve out spaciously. Conversely, a lightly cut and thin looking radial crease indicates a weaker sexual desire.

WEAK

STRONG

This line indicates how much sexual drive a person has. It does not, however, point out any tendency toward monogamy or infidelity. A person's expression of their sensuality will be heightened or diminished by the quality of this line. The degree of sensuality is directly proportionate to the depth and prominence of the line.

CHARACTERISTICS

More or Less:
Sexually Motivated
Sensually Expressive

SEX SYMBOLS

Hot: Mick Jagger • Angelina Jolie
Not: Don Knotts • Tipper Gore

Fun~Loving

*T*his upper transverse crease sculpts a curve as it makes its way to the base of the middle finger. This structure attests to a robust, fun loving spirit when around friends, and especially in an intimate relationship.

QUALITIES

These people are not afraid to ask for what they want. There's no beating around the bush; they know what they're looking for and everyone else is going to know it too. They have emotionally charged, excited spirits. They're compatible with those who are lively, animated and alert. Otherwise, they may quickly become bored. In their darker moments, they can be demanding and self-absorbed.

CHARACTERISTICS

Upbeat
Playful
Exciting
Lively

FAMOUS FUN-LOVERS

Mae West · Goldie Hawn
Drew Barrymore

39

Selfish

To check for self-centered-ness, confirm that the upper index finger segment is the shortest of the three. This disposition will be further pronounced if the apex bears a squarish, rather than a rounded or circular, formation.

QUALITIES

These are skeptical people who believe that things happen completely by chance. If this segment is very short, they may even lack morals, standards and values. At their worst, they are always looking out for Number One, shrugging accountability and ignoring the effects of their actions on others.

CHARACTERISTICS

Miserly
Ungenerous
Insensitive

FAMOUS MISERS

Imelda Marcos • Scrooge
Gordon Gecco

Demonstrative

*I*n general,
people with
upper transverse
creases that curve in
formation – regardless of
direction, depth or length –
are verbally and physically
demonstrative with
their feelings.

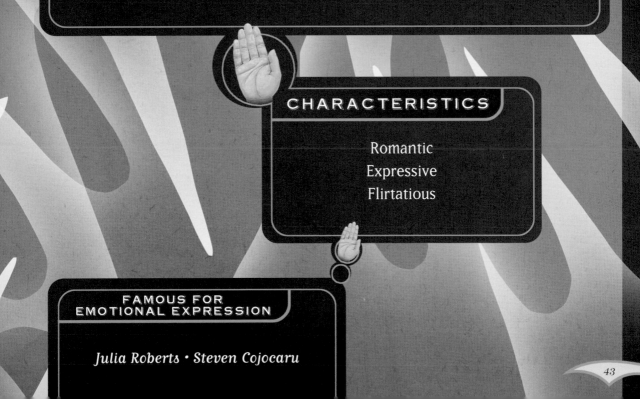

QUALITIES

These people have a clear channel to express their emotions. They make good counterparts to those who are emotionally reserved. However, if this line has a very pronounced curve, it could be too much of a good thing. In such instances, people constantly talk about what they feel and how they're experiencing life. The greater the curvature, the more likely they are to wear their heart on their sleeve.

CHARACTERISTICS

Romantic
Expressive
Flirtatious

FAMOUS FOR EMOTIONAL EXPRESSION

Julia Roberts • Steven Cojocaru

When the upper segment of the thumb is immoderately wide and thick, distinctly appearing top-heavy when compared to the rest of the thumb, a person's willpower is repeatedly used in a manipulative fashion.

If you're looking for someone who will take charge in a relationship, this may be the person for you. People with this feature are doers; they strive for results. They are motivated to shape their environment to meet their needs. Consequently, this quality is accompanied by a strong willpower, as well as drive and determination. It is the more evident, intense version of the "strong-willed" hand. People with this quality may, at times, prove difficult to reason with; they can be obstinate.

CHARACTERISTICS

Stubborn
High Expectations of Others
Demanding
Possessive

FAMOUS MANIPULATORS

Don King • Cleopatra
Nikita Khrushchev

I f the hypothenar region of the hand is flat, atrophied or generally characterless, it denotes a superficial, unreflective mind. A pad of flesh that is slightly upraised and moderately developed, by contrast, would indicate an adequate contemplative ability.

QUALITIES This feature of the hand reveals a tendency to follow the crowd and a reluctance to think critically. These are trendy people—you might say they're pop culture devotees. Their motto is: "If everyone's buying it, it's got to be good!" Their partners or friends could do them a favor by encouraging them to be more introspective and to question ideas and behaviors before accepting them as true or beneficial.

CHARACTERISTICS

Shallow
Materialistic
Conformist

FAMOUS FOR SUPERFICIALITY

Pamela Anderson • Jessica Simpson
Anna Nicole Smith • George Hamilton

Pessimistic

Note the commencement point of the medial transverse crease in relation to the radial arc crease. If the medial transverse crease begins below the radial arc crease, the element of pessimism will certainly play a role in one's demeanor and mental outlook.

QUALITIES

"It will never happen." "Quit while you're ahead." Statements like these are common for people with this imprint. Although subject to negative thinking, they are nonetheless pragmatists who look for the bottom line and avoid unnecessary risks. Their outlook stems from a subconscious desire to create security and stability; they are not quick to change. Unfortunately, they have a way of creating obstacles for themselves and may even discourage their partners from pursuing their dreams. What they really need is to learn how to enjoy what they already have!

CHARACTERISTICS

Critical
Judgmental
Paranoid (in extreme cases)
Cynical

FAMOUS PESSIMISTS

Woody Allen • Eeyore • Larry David

49

Philosophical

*T*he defini-
tive and
unerring
hallmark of the eternal
student is proclaimed
by the upper segment of
the middle finger. If it is the
longest of the three sections,
the owner is a deep thinker
and is blessed with a philo-
sophical mind.

These are definitely not shallow thinkers. Expect individuals with this marking to be quite introspective and reflective—not just about their own lives, but about the world outside as well. They delight in discussing many subjects ranging from world politics to conspiracy theories, from technology to sociology, and, of course, philosophy in general. These individuals are enlivened by the company of those who aspire for self-actualization.

CHARACTERISTICS

Curious
Enjoys Learning
Metaphysically Minded
Spiritual Seeker

FAMOUS PHILOSOPHERS

Socrates • Galileo
Madame Blavatsky • Dalai Lama

A hand in which the palm itself is slightly longer than it is square, united with fingers that are slightly short looking by comparison, reveals a person who has a fervent hunger to gratify their desires and emotions.

QUALITIES

Passionate people are intense and fiery. They strive to create personal independence and seek an adventurous life full of challenges. It's in their nature to crave excitement and attention. However, they may also be prone to abusing power and manipulating situations—sometimes out of sheer boredom! They are very good at starting projects and ventures, but not so skilled at maintaining them. They need others to manage their creations, so that they can continue to create.

CHARACTERISTICS

Dramatic
Zest For Life
Enthusiastic

FAMOUS FOR PASSION

Janis Joplin • Al Pacino
Elizabeth Taylor

53

Refined

*I*nspect the texture of the skin on the palm side of the hand. The degree of smoothness and softness will equal the degree of refinement and sensitivity found in the temperament. Smooth, silky skin reveals a cultured, well-mannered person, while a coarse or hard skin texture denotes a person of crude disposition.

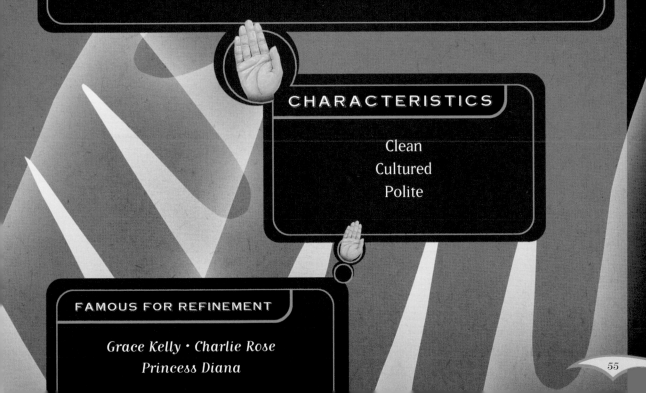

QUALITIES

This texture indicates a sophisticated and sensitive nature. These are warm people who really want the best for society. It pains them to witness social degradation. They're often inclined to help others elevate themselves or their immediate surroundings. Refined individuals avoid places where vulgar behavior or language can be found because it greatly disturbs them. They prefer to live in pleasant and attractive environments.

CHARACTERISTICS

Clean
Cultured
Polite

FAMOUS FOR REFINEMENT

Grace Kelly • Charlie Rose
Princess Diana

WORK

COOKING ABILITY

*T*he lower segment of the index finger reveals the interest and ability to participate in the world of food preparation. Upon inspection, it will clearly be the widest and thickest of the twelve finger sections. It is commonly the longest of the index segments as well.

When it comes to cooking, the wider the bottom segment of the index finger is, the more a person puts their heart into their tart. These people enjoy elegantly prepared, opulent and refined foods. They may also be indulgent and possess a strong urge to enjoy their senses.

CHARACTERISTICS

Food Lover
Culinary Artist

FAMOUS COOKS

Wolfgang Puck • Julia Childs
Emeril Lagasse

NATURE LOVER

*L*ook for a skin ridge pattern in the lower region of the hypothenar. In the sunlight or under a bright lamp, check for this "loop" that resembles a series of arches within one another. It is horizontally positioned, with the open end toward the edge of the palm. This mark evidences a special affinity for the countryside and forest.

Though not inherently hermits or loners, these individuals often withdraw from social interaction as they find working alongside others to be difficult. However, they will benefit from reflecting on their social exchanges. Their disposition makes them ideal candidates for careers in search and rescue, wildlife or wilderness research and surveying. Whatever the case, it would be wise to avoid giving a nature lover a desk job — it would never last!

CHARACTERISTICS

Outdoors Person
Comfortable In Solitude

FAMOUS NATURE LOVERS

John Muir • Jane Goodall
Henry David Thoreau

ADVENTUROUS

A person who craves physical adventure will have a hand in which the bottom part of the palm is slightly wider and broader than the top (where it meets the fingers). Notice also that the bottom edges will be thick and fleshy, and are most often rounded.

QUALITIES

This is the typical hand found on an archeologist, park ranger or firefighter. It shows a need for stimulation, exploration and physical challenges, preferably in the great outdoors. These are busy, energetic people who love their freedom. Nearly half of those demonstrating this characteristic have the potential to be good leaders, and will enjoy being in charge. This is another configuration ill suited for a paper-pushing desk job.

CHARACTERISTICS

Exploratory
Outdoors Person
Likes to Travel

FAMOUS ADVENTURERS

Charles Lindbergh • Amelia Earhart
Jacques Cousteau

A specific configuration involving both the upper and medial transverse creases indicates a person with strong personal opinions on most subjects. Departing from separate starting points, the two creases curve gently toward each other as they approach their closest proximity at the center of the palm.

QUALITIES

These people strongly believe in their opinions, and they can't figure out why everyone else hasn't reached the same conclusions yet. They are highly responsible; both emotion and intellect go into every decision they make. In short, this feature provides backbone and strength of character. Opinionated people need to be careful, however, of becoming inflexible. They would do well to learn how to relax (though it won't come easily). They are generally career-driven and make good writers, talk show hosts or even politicians.

CHARACTERISTICS

Individualistic
Potentially Inflexible
Strong-Minded

FAMOUS FOR STRONG OPINIONS

Bill O'Reilly • Howard Stern
Ann Coulter

HONEST

*O*bserve the entire length of the little finger from the back of the hand. The straighter the finger is formed, the more honest the individual will be in their affairs and communications.

QUALITIES

With this hand, honesty comes naturally. People exhibiting this quality can be trusted with your business and your money. If they make a mistake, say with a deadline or a bill, rest assured they'll tell you about it. Deception makes these individuals very uncomfortable.

CHARACTERISTICS

Trustworthy
Straightforward
Truthful

FAMOUS FOR HONESTY

Abraham Lincoln • Harriet Tubman
Sherron Watkins

DISHONEST

*L*ooking at the back of the hand, take note of the entire length of the little finger. The greater the degree of twisting, bending or crookedness observed in the finger, the greater the degree of dishonesty in that person's affairs and communications.

QUALITIES

People with crooked pinkies may stretch the truth to get what they want. Actually, this may serve them well in areas such as promotion, marketing and sales. They excel at selling, whether it's a product, an idea or themselves! The inherent danger is that they may get caught in a tangle of lies, or worse yet, may start believing their own lies. Their distortions are rooted in a lack of self-confidence and insecurity. They think: "If I'm honest, I won't be as effective or have as much impact. I'll be more successful if I embellish." And so they do!

CHARACTERISTICS

Duplicitous
Tendency To Lie
Stretches The Truth
Untrustworthy

INFAMOUS FOR DISHONESTY

Ken Lay • Stephen Glass • Linda Tripp

69

AMBITIOUS

*A*mbitious individuals are revealed by an index finger that has its middle segment as the longest of the three. This quality is even further accentuated if the segment is engraved with several vertical lines.

These are the "goal-oriented" people always sought out in the classified ads. They may be a lone wolf entrepreneur, or a "Rah! Rah!" team player. While they are highly motivated, they can also be scatterbrained and lose sight of their goals. Ideally, these types need to be able to focus on one goal at a time in order to be successful, otherwise all their goals may remain undone.

CHARACTERISTICS

Goal-Oriented
Accomplished
Motivated

FAMOUS FOR AMBITION

Anthony Robbins • Bill Gates
Meg Whitman

INDEPENDENT

*A*n indepen-dent dis-position is shown when the medial transverse crease begins slightly above and separated from the radial arc crease at the thumb side. Additionally, a significant amount of impulsiveness will always be present in conjunction with this self-assured nature.

QUALITIES

The need for autonomy motivates these individuals who feel confident in their capacity for self-motivation and direction. Even so, they're capable of being quite productive on behalf of others. They are spontaneous, if not occasionally rash, and as such tend to take a lot of risks. Starting up projects is no trouble for them, but sustaining them is another story. They may have difficulty with followthrough; if they sense another opportunity in the wings, they'll quickly abandon ship.

CHARACTERISTICS

Assertive
Freethinking
Confident

FAMOUS INDEPENDENTS

Ralph Nader • Mark Twain

A person who enjoys and is comfort-able with making decisions will have a me-dial transverse crease that completes its journey in the territory underneath the ring finger. This is a wonderful configuration because one's thinking process is a healthy balance of both subjectivity and objectivity.

These are the pragmatic managers and the team coaches who keep their minds in the here and now. Decision making, either for themselves or for others, comes naturally...and they trust those choices. As these individuals are characteristically firm, they may at times prove inflexible and unable to compromise. They'll be even more effective if they learn when it is appropriate to say when.

CHARACTERISTICS

Problem Solving
Leadership Qualities
Uncompromising

FAMOUS DECISION-MAKERS

Lee Iacocca • Margaret Thatcher
Madeleine Albright

VISIONARY

*T*he tips of
the fingers
identify
visionary thinkers. These
tapering tips, resembling a
Druid's hood, must appear
on at least two of the fingers.
Most commonly, they will be
the index and the little finger.
Additionally, if the thumb
also carries this type of tip, the
person is substantially idealistic
in their vision.

These inspirational motivators can sweep crowds off their feet. They should be working directly with the people, as opposed to pushing papers or toiling away on machinery and the like. Associates may be instrumental in helping them bring their vision into the realm of the tangible and concrete. The visionary personality may not always be grounded, and in some instances, could be a dreamer. If four or more tips are present on the hand, the individual's head is probably in the clouds.

CHARACTERISTICS

Idealistic
Inspirational
Intuitive

FAMOUS VISIONARIES

John Fitzgerald Kennedy
Henry Ford • Benjamin Franklin

STRONG-WILLED

A strong-willed individual can be recognized by a healthy formation of the thumb's upper segment. This padding (opposite the nail side) should feel firm, resilient and resemble the letter *D*. Similarly, if the padding looks flat and feels soft, the person will lack determination.

Perseverance and healthy determination characterize these strong-willed individuals. They don't give up; they see the folly in quitting. If a project fails, they're likely to pull themselves up by the bootstraps and go at it again, this time taking full advantage of their previous experience. Those whose thumbs are flat or without padding, however, may have difficulty holding on to their positions.

CHARACTERISTICS

Persistence
Single-Mindedness
Strong Character
Backbone

FAMOUS FOR STRONG WILL

Winston Churchill • Billy Jean King
Lance Armstrong

Check to see if the medial transverse crease is etched into the palm in a curved formation. The bearers of this configuration are predominantly right-brained thinkers. Inner experiences, feelings and instincts impact their perspectives and abilities.

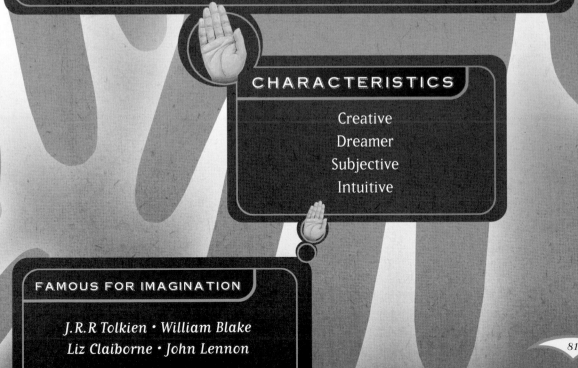

QUALITIES

Those with the imaginative engraving look at life as it could be, rather than how it actually is. Many possess an acute visual memory. They don't always think in a logical way, so they're capable of being quite original. They do well in occupations that encourage unorthodox thinking, such as advertising, design and architecture. These individuals may also be subject to melancholia or mood swings. They often view matters as far better or far worse than they really are. This quality is accentuated by a strongly curving line.

CHARACTERISTICS

Creative
Dreamer
Subjective
Intuitive

FAMOUS FOR IMAGINATION

J.R.R Tolkien • William Blake
Liz Claiborne • John Lennon

CREATIVE

Observing the palm side of the hand, compare the length of the ring finger with the index finger. Keep the fingers close together so that there are no spaces between them. If the ring finger is longer than the index finger, creativity is a constitutional feature.

QUALITIES

To those with a longer ring finger than index finger, self-expression and creativity are more important than financial gain, control over the work environment or having an influential position. They're not necessarily concerned with climbing the ladder of success, but rather, with their artistic and creative contributions.

CHARACTERISTICS

Artistic Temperament
Attentiveness To Appearance

FAMOUS CREATIVES

Beethoven • Michelangelo
Ella Fitzgerald

ANALYTICAL

Notice if the medial transverse crease is carved into the palm in a straight formation. If so, the bearers are predominantly left-brained thinkers, and their viewpoints are based upon the examination of facts and information. In addition, the straighter the line, the better at multitasking they are.

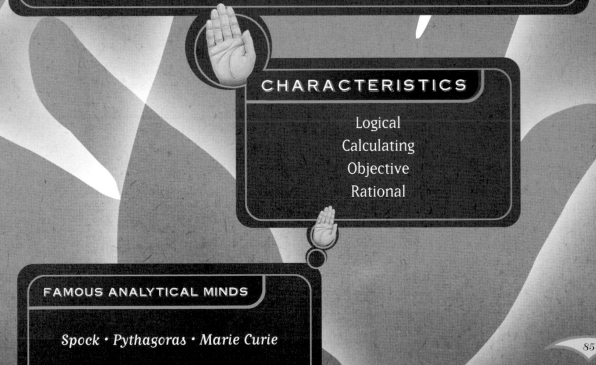

QUALITIES

"Just the facts, ma'am," would make a good motto for those with the analytical imprint. Their conclusions are based on hard data like statistics, as opposed to the subjective, often fluctuating opinions of their more emotionally driven counterparts. These are the type of people who might consider reading fiction a waste of time because they're looking for tangible gain from their efforts. They're generally good problem solvers, but may come off as emotionally cool or aloof, which is not necessarily true.

CHARACTERISTICS

Logical
Calculating
Objective
Rational

FAMOUS ANALYTICAL MINDS

Spock • Pythagoras • Marie Curie

85

INTELLIGENT

*L*ook to see if the medial transverse crease extends into the little finger section. This is the mark of a person who is endowed with an abundance of intelligence.

QUALITIES

Always curious, always asking questions, those who possess this formation love to know everything about everything. Ideal candidates for careers involving research or investigation, they are generally quite perceptive and exhibit solid deductive reasoning skills. The more the medial transverse crease extends to the ulnar side of the hand, the more they take the future into consideration when making decisions.

CHARACTERISTICS

Smart
Thoughtful
Curious

FAMOUS INTELLIGENTSIA

Albert Einstein • Stephen Hawking
Susan Sontag

MONEY-MAKING ABILITY

*N*otice if the medial transverse crease draws up slightly toward the little finger as it ends its journey. This signifies a marked ability and desire to make a considerable amount of money. In addition, a spirit of competitiveness frequently accompanies this contour.

QUALITIES

These ambitious people know the value of a dollar. They're efficient, resourceful and not inclined to waste money. They'll spend money when they need to, but normally only after shopping around enough to know they have absolutely secured the best deal. While good at managing what they have, they're also always looking to increase their wealth. They make excellent investors.

CHARACTERISTICS

Business Ability
Good With Money
Money-Minded

FAMOUS MONEY-MAKERS

Donald Trump • William Randolph Hearst • Carleton "Carly" Fiorina

COMMUNICATIVE

*T*he eager-
ness and
capability to
effectively communicate
are confirmed by the pres-
ence of the vertical ulnar
crease, which is positioned
on the palm directly below
the little finger. This line also
indicates a strong inclination
to express one's views and
ideas, especially if the crease
is substantial in length.

QUALITIES

A crease that is clear and clean will impart a good measure of confidence, creativity and self-expression. Both the desire and the ability to write are concomitant factors of this feature. This crease does not have to be as deeply cut as the other lines on the hand in order to bestow its good qualities.

CHARACTERISTICS

Talkative
Expressive
Interactive

FAMOUS COMMUNICATORS

Oprah Winfrey • Larry King
Terry Gross

HARD-WORKING

A person who is hard-working and responsible by nature will have a middle finger that has a longer middle segment than the other two. In addition, a few vertical lines inscribed on this section will heighten these qualities even further, possibly denoting a workaholic.

92   WORK

QUALITIES

Hard-working individuals use their time efficiently as good planners, organizers and resource managers. On projects, they are diligent, focused and committed to applying themselves fully. They make sure what needs to be accomplished gets accomplished. To their detriment, they are prone to sacrificing relationships with friends and family in the name of their career. Their motto is: "There is pride and honor in work."

CHARACTERISTICS

Industrious
Conscientious
Career-Driven

FAMOUS HARD WORKERS

Henry Ford • Dale Carnegie
Walt Disney

TEAM PLAYER

Check to see if the medial transverse crease makes its way adjoined with the radial arc crease for a short distance at its commencement. These are people who prefer collaborating and interacting with co-contributors.

Team players feel most at home working cooperatively within a group, team or regular network. They like to share and express opinions while getting feedback from others. In this way they are able to seek acknowledgement and validation in business ventures. They can be self-conscious at times, worrying what other people think about their plans and ideas.

CHARACTERISTICS

Takes Calculated Risks
Conservative in Business Ventures
Enjoys Interacting with Colleagues
Cautious

FAMOUS TEAM PLAYERS

Quincy Jones • Ronald Reagan

A NOTE FROM THE AUTHOR

Although this is not a palmistry course book, I am confident that the reader, through application of this material, will certainly recognize the veracity and usefulness of hand analysis. The life purpose of a human being is clearly written into the hand. Through it one can gain a comprehensive understanding of a person's emotional, creative, career and spiritual directions. Palmistry is a most fascinating study and I encourage the reader to further investigate and explore this great science. Learning to read hands is enjoyable and it is a powerful tool that can help people. In the words of the renowned American palmist, Dr. William G. Benham, "Palmistry is a study worthy of the best efforts of the best minds."

Vernon Mahabal
DIRECTOR
The Palmistry Institute
www.palmistryinstitute.com